PICTURE OF ME

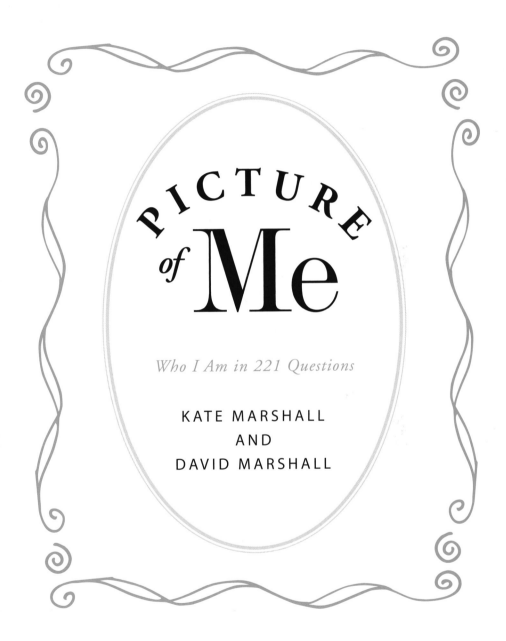

PICTURE *of* Me

Who I Am in 221 Questions

KATE MARSHALL

AND

DAVID MARSHALL

BROADWAY BOOKS   NEW YORK

Published in the United States by Broadway Books, an imprint of The
Doubleday Publishing Group, a division of Random House, Inc., New York.
www.broadwaybooks.com

BROADWAY BOOKS and its logo, a letter B bisected on the diagonal, are trademarks
of Random House, Inc.

Book design by Ellen Cipriano

Library of Congress Cataloging-in-Publication Data

Marshall, Kate, 1959–
Picture of me : who I am in 221 questions / Kate Marshall and
David Marshall. — 1st ed.
p. cm.
1. Self—Miscellanea.   I. Marshall, David, 1956–   II. Title.

BF697.M37   2009
155.2—dc22
2008030624

ISBN 978–0–7679–3037–6

PRINTED IN THE UNITED STATES OF AMERICA

1 3 5 7 9 10 8 6 4 2

First Edition

CONTENTS

My name: _____

Age: _____

Current month and year: _____

Why I'm writing in this book:

___ just for fun—I love this stuff

___ to mark this moment in my life

___ to answer the big question, "Who am I?," in bite-sized pieces

___ to give my life a little checkup—what's working, what's not

___ so I can reread this in a few years to see what has (or hasn't) changed

___ to show it to someone I'd like to know me better

___ so my future great-grandchildren can see what my life was like

___ other _____

PRIVACY NOTICE

!

Who has permission to read my *Picture of Me*?

___ just me, please!

___ anyone—I'm an open book

___ these people: _____

_____

_____

Me (photo, drawing, stick figure, cartoon . . .):

ℒ

My Physical Self

Basic stats:

height _____   natural hair color _____

shoe size _____   current hair color _____

eye color _____   blood type _____

skin color _____   lefty or righty _____

I look like this famous person or cartoon character: _____

_____

I *wish* I looked like this person: _____

_____

My three best features:

1. _____

2. _____

3. _____

I've been blessed (or cursed) with these physical traits (blue eyes, allergies, tallness, pointy nose, curly hair, athleticism, big feet . . .):

_____

_____

_____

Other physical features that I've picked up along the way (scars, tattoos, six-pack abs, double chin . . .): _____

_____

_____

If I could change anything about my body I'd: _____

_____

_____

To get me going in the morning, I need:

    ___ nothing—I wake up ready to go!   ___ a refreshing shower
    ___ coffee, lots and lots of coffee   ___ other _____
    ___ exercise

TRUE OR FALSE

I'm a vegetarian T/F

I'm always on a diet T/F

I'm always hungry T/F

I eat quickly T/F

I hardly ever get sick T/F

I'm coordinated T/F

I've got rhythm T/F

I can whistle T/F

I'm ticklish T/F

I can touch my tongue to my
   nose T/F

I can *rrrrr*roll my R's T/F

I can touch my toes T/F

I wear contacts or glasses T/F

I often take naps T/F

I'm a night owl T/F

I snore T/F

I talk in my sleep T/F

I photograph well T/F

I bite my nails T/F

I sunburn easily T/F

I floss regularly T/F

I practically never pass gas T/F

I hate being hot T/F

My hands or feet are always
   cold T/F

I get queasy in cars or on
   boats T/F

I have to pee often T/F

I'm losing my hair T/F

I've found gray hairs T/F

If so, I pluck or color them T/F

I have a pleasant voice T/F

I have a loud laugh T/F

My favorite:

breakfast food _____

sandwich _____

hot food _____

cold food _____

take-out food _____

pizza topping(s) _____

snack _____

sinful snack _____

fruit _____

vegetable _____

bread _____

pasta _____

meat _____

dessert _____

spice _____

hot drink _____

cold drink _____

other food _____

If I could eat anything I wanted for a week, with no ill effects, I'd eat nothing but:

   __ junk food—the saltier, the fattier, the better
   __ desserts—"Sweet Tooth" is my middle name
   __ salads and veggies—call me crazy, but I love the stuff
   __ everything—I just love to eat, *period*
   __ whatever—food isn't that important to me
   __ other _____

weight _____   dress/shirt size _____   pant size _____

How I feel about my weight and size:

   __ darn proud   __ embarrassed (those sizes may be a wee
   __ satisfied   bit of wishful thinking)
   __ not satisfied   __ other _____
   __ don't care

On *weekdays,* I usually sleep from _____ to _____.

I feel rested when I wake up (Y/Sort of/N)

On *weekends,* I usually sleep from _____ to _____.

I feel rested when I wake up (Y/Sort of/N)

Health issues (allergies, aches and pains . . .): _____

_____

_____

_____

_____

_____

My least healthy habit(s):_____

_____

_____

_____

_____

_____

ON A SCALE OF 1–5:	1 = PRACTICALLY NONEXISTENT
	5 = AMAZINGLY HIGH

my fitness level is _____   my strength is _____
my flexibility is _____   my motivation to get more
fit is _____

In a typical week, I do these exercises:

WHAT   HOW LONG/HOW OFTEN

_____   _____

_____   _____

_____   _____

_____   _____

I'd exercise more if: _____

_____

_____

_____

_____

_____

_____

I'd love to be able to:

    __ dunk a basketball   __ hike_____

    __ do a cartwheel   __ lift_____

    __ run a __-minute mile   __ juggle _____

    __ finish a marathon   __ learn to_____

    __ swim the _____   __ avoid the gym at all costs

    __ do ___ push-ups   __ other_____

    __ dance like _____

Overall, I'm satisfied with my health and body T/F

If not, I'd be satisfied if: _____

_____

_____

_____

_____

_____

INSIDE OUT

My Personality

These are some of my best qualities (circle words that *do* describe you and underline words you *wish* described you):

ambitious	fair	philosophical
calm	flexible	playful
cautious	friendly	practical
clever	funny	punctual
colorful	generous	quirky
compassionate	gentle	realistic
confident	honest	respectful
considerate	humble	responsible
creative	intellectual	smart
curious	kindhearted	spontaneous
dependable	lively	spunky
determined	nurturing	steady
direct	optimistic	trusting
discreet	passionate	wise
easygoing	patient	other _____

A few words that describe my worst qualities: _____

_____

_____

If a kindergarten teacher watched me now, she or he would report this about me:

E = EXCELLENT	S = SATISFACTORY	N = NEEDS IMPROVEMENT

___ makes friends easily   ___ cleans up after self

___ plays well with others   ___ takes turns nicely

___ stays on task   ___ has neat handwriting

___ sits still at circle time   ___ follows directions well

___ shares toys   ___ other _____

Comments: _____

_____

_____

_____

My "dog personality" is a:

___ Golden Retriever—trusting, eager-to-please, hate being
    alone

___ Jack Russell Terrier—brave, spunky (*Hey, did you just call
    me "hyper"?*)

___ Labrador—love to eat, play, and hang out with friends,
    good with kids

___ Poodle—smart, lively, oh-so-stylish and proud of my
    pedigree

___ Rottweiler—protective, determined, misunderstood

___ Bearded Collie—bouncy, curious, often silly, sometimes
    bossy

___ Border Collie—eager, obsessively hardworking, definitely
    Type A

___ English Bulldog—homebody, some say lazy but I say
    m-e-l-l-o-w

___ German Shepherd—can be aloof with strangers, but loyal
    to friends and family

___ Whippet—gentle, shy, affectionate

I'm more afraid than the average person of (spiders, needles, heights,
public speaking . . .): _____

_____

_____

_____

I feel proud when: _____

_____

_____

I get excited when: _____

_____

_____

I feel grateful that: _____

_____

_____

I'm embarrassed when: _____

_____

_____

It ticks me off when: _____

_____

_____

It makes me sad when: _____

_____

_____

I'm playful and spontaneous T/F   I make decisions and stick to
I love a good, heated debate T/F   them T/F
I relish being different T/F   I'm high-maintenance T/F
I stay calm under pressure T/F   I'm superstitious T/F
I'm affectionate T/F   I only say "I'm sorry" if I really
I easily express my feelings T/F   mean it T/F
I want things to be perfect T/F   I process things by talking T/F

My astrological sign is: _____

What they say about people with this sign is:

___ totally true for me; I am the poster child for this sign
___ totally not true for me
___ partly true for me, especially the part about _____

_____

___ I don't know enough about astrology to say
___ hogwash—I don't believe in astrology

For maximum sanity and happiness, I need a whole lot of:

___ time with friends	___ exercise
___ time with _____	___ feeling useful
___ time alone	___ money
___ sunshine	___ pride in my work
___ the beach	___ pride in my home
___ open space	___ travel
___ great food	___ team/community bonding
___ chocolate	___ creative happenings
___ sleep	___ intellectual stimulation
___ attention	___ books
___ laughter	___ music
___ love and affection	___ other _____
___ sex	

GET OUT OF JAIL FREE

THIS GET OUT OF JAIL FREE CARD ENTITLES ME TO A FREE PASS FOR THE CRIME OF:

Ticket to

PARADISE

Reserved for _____ (name of traveler)

Choose two itinerary options for your stay in Paradise:

___ huge shopping mall where everything is free

___ all-you-can-eat buffet; delicious and calorie-free

___ beautiful, friendly people and non-stop _____

___ quality time with _____

___ relaxing at the _____

___ adventure outing to _____

___ time travel to _____

___ other _____

OUTSIDE IN

My Sense of Style

Overall, the personal style I'm going for is:

___ natural, outdoorsy	___ earthy	___ tough or dangerous
___ athletic	___ funky/artsy	___ who thinks about
___ neat, presentable	___ cute	this stuff?
___ chic, elegant	___ practical	___ other _____
___ sexy	___ effortless	
___ hip	___ intelligent	

I pay close attention to my personal appearance and style T/F
I care if others see me as reasonably attractive T/F
I am better-looking now than I was five years ago T/F

I look best in these colors: _____

_____

I've gotten compliments on my appearance when I: _____

_____

ON A "HOTNESS" SCALE OF 1–10:	1 = UGH
	5 = AVERAGE
	10 = OOH BABY!

I'd give myself a _____

_____

My friends might give me a _____

_____

My love interest would probably give me a _____

_____

My hair style (length, cut, challenges . . .): _____

_____

My favorite:

shampoo _____

deodorant _____

skin care or makeup product _____

scented or flavored product _____

_____ I don't have favorites: I just use whatever's cheap, on sale,
or handy

My favorite outfit (draw, describe, or attach a photo):

When I shop for clothes, I'm looking for things that are:

___ inexpensive

___ on sale or a really good value (why pay full price?)

___ comfortable, *period*

___ practical (go with everything, hide stains, machine washable . . .)

___ flattering (make me look fabulous)

___ the latest fashion

___ high quality design, brand, or material, no matter the price

The last time I bought shoes or a piece of clothing (what, where, when): _____

_____

_____

_____

If a rich uncle granted me a total wardrobe makeover, I'd buy: _____

_____

_____

_____

_____

_____

The family I grew up with (photo or drawing of
important family members and pets):

Names and ages: _____

_____

_____

The family I chose (photo or drawing of spouse,
significant other, kids, pets, etc.):

Names and ages: _____

_____

_____

FAMILY PORTRAIT

My Family

My family is from: _____

I consider myself (race, ethnicity, class, or other): _____

My grandparents' first language was: _____

Language(s) in the home I grew up in: _____

In my home now we speak: _____

My family is like:

___ a warm, sunny day—pleasant

___ a three-ring circus—odd but entertaining

___ a disaster scene—walking wounded

___ a refrigerator—a tad chilly

___ warm cocoa—sweet and comforting

___ the Kennedys—high achievers

___ a soap opera—*d-r-a-m-a!*

___ this TV family _____

___ other _____

These additional people are so close that they feel like family (family friend, godparent . . .): _____

Briefly, here's what key family members are up to:

_____ (name), my _____ (relationship)

Where living _____

Activity or interest _____

_____ (name), my _____ (relationship)

Where living _____

Activity or interest _____

_____ (name), my _____ (relationship)

Where living _____

Activity or interest _____

_____ (name), my _____ (relationship)

Where living _____

Activity or interest _____

My pet _____ (name of pet)

Kind of animal: _____

Age and physical description:_____

_____

Personality, talents, or quirks: _____

_____

Another pet _____ (name of pet)

Kind of animal: _____

Age and physical description:_____

_____

Personality, talents, or quirks: _____

_____

Other important animals in my life: _____

_____

_____

My role in the family is usually to be the:

__ ATM machine
__ peacemaker
__ troublemaker
__ quiet one
__ communicator
__ organizer
__ breadwinner
__ benevolent dictator
__ moral compass
__ nurturer
__ cheerleader

__ black sheep
__ rebel
__ achiever
__ baby
__ princess
__ chauffeur
__ maid
__ entertainer/joker
__ softy
__ other _____

Over the next year, I'll try to be more _____ (what) toward _____ (whom).

I can best count on this family member to:

remember my birthday _____

plan gatherings and holidays _____

spend time with me _____

make things fun _____

handle an emergency _____

make me feel loved _____

cheer me up _____

teach me _____

psychoanalyze me _____

brag about me _____

spoil me _____

light a fire under me _____

give/loan me money _____

I'm especially thankful to _____ (family member) for:

_____

_____

_____

This is the family member I'd most like to:

have a good year _____

win the lottery _____

find true love _____

see more of _____

borrow clothes from _____

challenge to a game or race _____

slap upside the head _____

give a makeover to _____

buy something for _____

spend a day alone with _____

get closer to _____

take care of _____

make up with _____

say "I love you" to _____

These are my best friends (photo, drawing, or memento):

Names: _____

_____

_____

PLAYMATES

My Friends

Best female friend(s): _____
Best male friend(s): _____

Best single friend: _____   Oldest friend: _____
Best married/attached   Newest friend: _____
  friend: _____

These are (or were) my closest friends from my:

childhood _____

job _____

volunteer work _____

school _____

neighborhood _____

place of worship _____

sports/clubs _____

hobby _____

other _____

What I love or appreciate about my closest friends:

1. _____ : _____

_____

2. _____ : _____

_____

3. _____ : _____

_____

What I think they like about me: _____

_____

_____

_____

On a typical weekend, you'll find my friends and me: _____

_____

_____

_____

Friends I can best count on to:

go shopping with me _____

exercise with me _____

meet me for a drink or dinner _____

just hang out with me _____

fill in as a date _____

cheer me up _____

flirt with me _____

know the answer _____

give good directions _____

give fashion advice _____

give relationship advice _____

understand me _____

listen _____

tell the truth _____

keep a secret _____

inspire me _____

know the right people _____

dish the gossip _____

pick up the check _____

do me a favor _____

Word-friend associations:

coffee _____		computer _____	
beer _____		book _____	
holiday card _____		text message _____	
diet _____		puppy _____	
car _____		party _____	
kids _____		hat _____	
summer _____		$ _____	
music _____		#*%@ _____	
joke _____		XXX _____	

I'd like to be better friends with: _____

I miss having this person as a friend: _____

I'm usually the friend who:

___ makes people laugh	___ is fashionably late
___ can keep a secret	___ remembers birthdays
___ knows the latest	___ handles the money
___ listens to problems	___ loans things or money
___ gives good advice	___ throws the party
___ stands up for you	___ is the designated driver
___ tells it like it is	___ is a handy platonic date
___ introduces people	___ can fix things
___ plans get-togethers	___ other _____

SEEKING FRIENDSHIP

Looking for a friend who is:

_____

For (kind of activities, support . . .):

_____

_____

_____

LOVE & LUST

My Love Life

I love myself, warts and all T/F
I have been in love with someone T/F

I am:

___ heterosexual   ___ transgender
___ bisexual   ___ unsure or exploring
___ homosexual   ___ other _____
___ asexual   ___ as if I'd write it here
___ polyamorous

About my sex life or sexual orientation I am:

___ 100% open and willing to dish   ___ discreet
___ open with friends or family   ___ very, very private

I admire this couple's relationship: _____

I have a celebrity crush on: _____

The movie version of my love life:

Title: _____ , rated _____

Starring _____ as me, and _____

Genre (circle one): comedy/drama/soap opera/mystery/documentary/
cartoon/tragedy

It starts off with: _____

_____

_____

_____

And in the end: _____

_____

_____

_____

_____

If Single

I am single right now because:

    ___ I love being single and am having fun with it
    ___ I'm way too _____ for a relationship right now
    ___ I'm recovering from a breakup
    ___ the right person hasn't come along yet, but it's okay
    ___ It's not for lack of trying; I'd love to be in a good
        relationship right now
    ___ other _____

For now I want:

    ___ to be by myself for a while
    ___ strictly companionship
    ___ just sex, no strings
    ___ a relationship that's meaningful but not necessarily forever
    ___ true love and commitment
    ___ other _____

When I first meet someone, I'm often attracted to this physical type:

_____

_____

_____

A deal breaker for me when I meet someone is (bad breath, talking about ex, smoking . . .): _____

_____

_____

_____

The most important personal qualities I'd want in a partner are: _____

_____

_____

_____

I've got my eye on this person (or people): _____

_____

_____

_____

My last relationship was with _____

It lasted _____

What was good about us: _____

_____

_____

What wasn't so great about us: _____

_____

_____

Why we broke up: _____

_____

_____

I'm over it:

___ yes

___ no

___ almost

___ actually, I've never had what I'd call a relationship

I sometimes wonder about someone I once let get away T/F

I usually know pretty quickly if I like someone or not T/F

I prefer to be friends before lovers T/F

I'm often the one who makes the first move T/F

I need to be very physically attracted to someone to proceed T/F

I don't want to know everything right away—I like a little mystery T/F

I don't believe in open relationships—one person at a time, please T/F

I admit to being rather high-maintenance in relationships (but I'm worth it!) T/F

I find the whole dating thing (check all that apply):

___ fun, actually   ___ boring
___ entertaining   ___ awkward
___ interesting   ___ a necessary evil
___ useful   ___ a waste of time
___ stressful   ___ NA/I'm not dating
___ disappointing   ___ who dates anymore?
___ baffling

I find the whole "hookup" thing:

___ glorious   ___ confusing—someone always gets hurt
___ okay for now   ___ unthinkable

I have tried or would consider meeting people by:

___ meeting friends of my   ___ dating a coworker or
    friends   customer
___ blind dates   ___ joining an organization
___ Internet dating   for singles
___ going to a bar or club   ___ other_____
___ dating a friend's ex

If in a Relationship

I am in a relationship with:_____

We are:

    ___ nonexclusive   ___ engaged

    ___ exclusive   ___ married

    ___ very committed   ___ other _____

We've been together (since when or for how long): _____

_____

How we met: _____

_____

_____

_____

I first fell for this person because: _____

_____

_____

My love interest (photo, drawing, or other portrayal):

Name: _____

We see each other:

___ every day—we live
    together
___ almost every day
___ a couple of times a week
___ about once a week

___ a few times a month
___ not often enough—we're
    long-distance
___ other _____

Recent milestone(s) in our relationship (spent the night, said "I love you," anniversary, moved in together . . .): _____

_____

_____

_____

_____

A time capsule with souvenirs from our time together so far would hold: _____

_____

_____

_____

_____

Three things I adore or appreciate about this person:

1. _____

2. _____

3. _____

Three things I love doing together:

1. _____

2. _____

3. _____

The best thing about us as a couple is: _____

_____

The biggest challenge to our relationship is: _____

_____

It would help our love life if I:

stopped _____

started _____

WHERE I LIVE

My Home

Who else lives here (people and animals): _____

_____

_____

_____

The monthly rent or mortgage is $_____ , and my
share of that is $_____ .

I'd describe my home decor as:

  __ decor? What's that?   __ All-American
  __ a mixed bag—truly eclectic   __ traditional
  __ funky, thrift-store chic   __ transitional
  __ ethnic/international   __ contemporary
  __ your basic dorm room   __ Southwestern
  __ a pigsty   __ country
  __ a work-in-progress   __ other _____

This is my home (photo or sketch of
what it looks like on the outside):

A sketch of the floor plan of my house or apartment:

Common smells in my home: _____

_____

Common sounds in my home: _____

_____

Overall, the best room in my house is: _____

This is what I like about it: _____

_____

_____

This is my favorite place at home to:

watch TV _____   reflect on life_____

talk on the phone _____   curl up with a book_____

listen to music _____   take a nap _____

eat dinner _____   look out the window_____

hang out with friends or   other _____
   family _____

My house (or room) is:

___ clean, but disheveled—the floor under all those piles is
     spotless, I swear
___ dirty, but organized—everything filed, folded, and put
     away; just don't get out the white gloves
___ both clean and organized, thank you very much
___ both dirty and disheveled—but I'm still a good person

On (or in) my bedside table I keep: _____

_____

Favorite thing hanging on the wall: _____

_____

Favorite family heirloom: _____

_____

Favorite childhood keepsake: _____

_____

My neighborhood is (check all that apply):

___ safe   ___ friendly

___ affordable   ___ good for kids

___ wealthy   ___ attractive

___ middle class   ___ changing a lot

___ working class   ___ close to jobs

___ lively   ___ close to shopping

___ quiet   ___ close to entertainment

___ mostly young   ___ where my friends are

___ mostly old   ___ generally awful

___ ethnically diverse   ___ wonderful—I'm staying

My neighbors: _____

_____

Shops or restaurants I go to a lot: _____

_____

Best thing about my neighborhood or town: _____

_____

GETTING THINGS DONE

Work, School, and Other Duties

I am (check all that apply):

___ working full-time   ___ a volunteer
___ working part-time   ___ a parent
___ self-employed   ___ a homemaker
___ job hunting   ___ a caretaker (of family members)
___ a full-time student ___ retired
___ a part-time student ___ other _____

Overall, I'd say the work/nonwork balance in my life is:

___ too much work or study, I'd like more time for (relaxing, family . . .)_____

___ about right for now

___ not enough work or study, I could use more (money, stimulation, credits . . .)_____

My work (picture of workplace, school, coworkers, business card, school brochure . . .):

School(s) I've been to: _____ _____

Classes or major: _____ _____

When I graduated: _____ _____

Degree or certificate: _____ _____

Other education: _____ _____

Where I work: _____ Salary: _____

My job title: _____ Hours/week: _____

Basically, what I do in my job is: _____

_____

_____

_____

Volunteer or other duties that are important to me: _____

_____

_____

_____

I chose _____ (job, school, or activity) because:

__ of its great location

__ it has a top-notch
reputation

__ it makes me happy
(most of the time)

__ it's fun and/or rewarding

__ I'm learning a lot

__ I'm good at it

__ it's what I need to do in
order to _____

__ it's helping people or a
cause

__ I like the people

__ the money is good

__ I like the perks and benefits

__ the hours work well for me

__ it's a family tradition

__ I didn't have much of a
choice

__ other _____

PERFORMANCE REVIEW

Here's the honest performance review I'd give myself for my work as a

_____ (student, employee, parent, or volunteer):

1 = TERRIBLE   5 = FABULOUS

___ How well I collaborate with others
___ How well I communicate my ideas in writing
___ How well I communicate my ideas verbally
___ How insightful or creative I am
___ How thorough or accurate I am
___ How much I participate and take on additional tasks
___ How well I manage my time
___ How organized I am
___ How hard I try
___ How reliably I show up and get the job done
___ Other _____
___ Overall _____

What I *do* like about what I'm doing: _____

_____

_____

_____

What I *don't* like about what I'm doing: _____

_____

_____

_____

My dream job would be: _____

_____

_____

_____

If I didn't need to work for money I would: _____

_____

_____

_____

If people have true gifts or callings:

___ I haven't found mine yet
___ mine might have to do with _____
___ I know mine is _____

Five years from now I want to be:

___ working at _____
___ running my own _____
___ a parent
___ a stay-at-home parent
___ studying _____
___ volunteering for _____
___ helping to _____
___ done with _____
___ retired
___ other _____

FINANCIAL PICTURE

Money

If someone gave me $1,000 to spend in one weekend, I'd: _____

_____

If I won $1 million in the lottery this year, I'd: _____

_____

If I could give $100,000 to anyone in the world (other than myself or my family), I'd give it to: _____

For $ _____, I'd hang out with someone I hated, weekly for a year.

For $ _____, I'd dye my hair green for a month.

For $ _____, I'd say something that deeply hurt my friend's feelings.

For $ _____, I'd give up all sex for a year.

For $ _____, I'd agree to vote for someone I didn't respect.

For $ _____ per year, I'd work in a job I hated for five years.

For $ _____, I'd marry someone I didn't love.

I am financially:

___ self-sufficient—I support myself
___ a team with _____; we each
     contribute and support each other
___ not quite self-sufficient—I get some help from _____

_____

___ totally supported by _____

I consider myself (or my family):

___ poor	___ well-off
___ working class	___ lucky
___ middle class	___ other _____
___ upper middle class	

My friends and I have similar spending habits T/F

My significant other (or housemate) makes:

___ more money than I do
___ less money than I do
___ about the same as I do
___ I don't know

We usually agree on what we can and cannot afford T/F

When we disagree about money, it's usually concerning: _____

_____

_____

I regularly spend a significant amount of money on:

___ groceries
___ eating out
___ coffee shops
___ rent/mortgage
___ home repair/remodeling
___ home decor
___ credit card interest
___ phone/utilities
___ Internet/cable
___ car payment/repair
___ gas and tolls
___ bus/train commute
___ school fees
___ books
___ work clothes
___ play clothes
___ jewelry
___ lingerie
___ gifts

___ charity/tithing
___ fitness/health club
___ health care
___ computers/gadgets
___ vacations
___ day/weekend trips
___ hobbies
___ bars/clubs
___ movies/shows
___ other tickets
___ kids' activities
___ babysitter/day care
___ other family members
___ pets
___ music
___ videos/games
___ other "toys"
___ other _____

I make $ _____ per year.

My family makes $ _____ per year.

The most expensive thing I own: _____

Assets (investments, home, car, other): _____

_____

_____

_____

Debt (mortgage, car, credit card, student, other): _____

_____

_____

_____

My expenses are in line with my income T/F

I make a budget T/F

I usually stick to the budget T/F/NA

I'm a thrifty shopper T/F

I pay off my bills every month T/F

I put money into savings every month T/F

I've made some good investments T/F

I'm well-informed about personal finance T/F

I have health insurance T/F

I'd be financially better off if I spent less money on: _____

_____

I'd be financially better off if I made more money by: _____

_____

I donate money to: _____

_____

When it comes to money, I worry:

    __ constantly   __ every once in a while

    __ often   __ not one little bit

My happiness is:

    __ not at all tied to money

    __ somewhat tied to money

    __ really affected by money

Over the next ____ year(s), my goals are to:

save enough for _____

pay off my _____

be earning _____

other _____

WHERE I STAND

My Beliefs

Force yourself to pick a side:

Only thin women should wear bikinis T/F

People should try their best to fit in and act normal T/F

Online socializing counts as human interaction T/F

I'm going to Heaven when I die T/F

Chewing gum makes you look stupid T/F

Men and women act differently due to biology, not upbringing T/F

Love at first sight is usually 99% lust T/F

English Literature is a useful college major T/F

Everything happens for a reason T/F

I can make a difference T/F

Homosexuals don't choose to be homosexual; it's biological T/F

All babies are adorable T/F

If you think a law is unfair, it's okay to break it T/F

Acupuncture is a sensible option for treating pain T/F

It's wrong to have sex with someone you're not in love with T/F

Parents should let teens try alcohol with them, at home T/F

There is too much sex and violence on TV—government should limit it T/F

Americans are getting dumber T/F

People over sixty shouldn't have sex T/F

Psychotherapy is a waste of time and money T/F

People who have an affair should tell their spouse about it T/F

Racism in this country makes it very difficult for people of color to succeed T/F

The world was created in six days T/F

Smoking marijuana frequently leads to other drug use T/F

Dogs are better pets than cats T/F

Life begins at conception T/F

There is one perfect person for everyone T/F

People are poor because they aren't trying hard enough T/F

Criticizing the president's policies is unpatriotic T/F

Making cell phone calls in a restaurant is rude T/F

Marriage is forever, for better or worse T/F

I believe in:

fate Y/N   angels Y/N
karma Y/N   ghosts Y/N
luck Y/N   life on other planets Y/N

I support:

health coverage for absolutely everyone Y/N

deporting all illegal immigrants Y/N

a woman's right to end her pregnancy for any reason Y/N

assisted suicide for terminally ill patients who want it Y/N

affirmative action for minorities' jobs and education Y/N

the death penalty Y/N

legal marriage for same-sex couples Y/N

strict controls on gun ownership Y/N

legal sale of sexual services for money Y/N

legal sale of marijuana for medical purposes Y/N

I follow politics closely T/F

I am registered to vote T/F

I voted in the last general election T/F

I voted for _____ in the last presidential election.

I'd love to see _____ as president someday.

ON A SCALE OF 1 (NOT AT ALL) TO 5 (PASSIONATELY), I AM INTERESTED IN EVENTS RELATED TO:

___ the earth/environment
___ foreign policy
___ my country
___ my state

___ my county/town
___ my friends/family
___ myself
___ other _____

I get news from (which newspaper, website, person, station . . .): _____

_____

_____

_____

Overall, I am politically (mark an "X" along the scale):

|————————————————|————————————————|
very liberal   moderate   very conservative

If I had to choose, I'd pick a government that:

___ is small and lets people and companies manage their own
     affairs
___ gets involved in protecting the little guy and working for
     the greater good

I connect best with the:

___ Democratic Party   ___ Libertarian Party
___ Republican Party   ___ other _____
___ Green Party   ___ not sure

These are some politicians I respect (dead or alive): _____

_____

_____

_____

_____

The government's top five priorities should be to:

___ ensure national security
___ manage immigration into this country
___ protect our freedoms of speech, privacy, and assembly
___ take care of the poor, elderly, disabled, and other
    vulnerable groups
___ create jobs and a strong economy
___ provide quality education
___ ensure quality health care
___ keep law and order
___ encourage scientific and industrial innovations
___ support human rights, here and abroad
___ promote peace and democracy in the world
___ protect and preserve land, sea, sky, and wildlife
___ other _____

Violence and war are necessary:

___ never; violence is morally wrong and never solves anything
___ only when being attacked
___ rarely; peaceful solutions can usually be found through
    skillful dialogue and conflict resolution
___ sometimes; force may be the only way to implement
    justice or get what you need
___ often; unfortunately, violence is usually the only language
    that's universally understood

I'm passionate about supporting this cause: _____

What this country or world needs now is: _____

On a scale of 1–5 (where 1 = terrified and 5 = optimistic), when
thinking about this country's future I am _____

Faith or spirituality is an important part of my life Y/N

I was raised as a _____ (religion) and now consider myself:

___ this religion _____
___ religious, but not affiliated
___ spiritual, but not formally religious
___ agnostic
___ atheist
___ other _____

I believe in a higher power or presence Y/N/Unsure

If so, I call this presence: _____

And describe it as: _____

_____

_____

I credit (or blame) religion for: _____

_____

_____

_____

FAQ

Random Stuff

My signature: _____

Nicknames people call me: _____

My phone numbers: _____

My email addresses: _____

My IM or other screen names: _____

My blogs or online social networks: _____

_____

Languages I speak: _____

Hobby or obsession: _____

Special or hidden talent: _____

Embarrassing or gross habit: _____

Some of the best music I've been listening to lately: _____

_____

_____

_____

_____

_____

I can't stand this music: _____

_____

_____

_____

I get music from (which radio station, download site, or other source):

_____

_____

I play music on (MP3, radio, computer, or other player): _____

_____

The soundtrack to my life would have these songs on it:

	LOVE THIS	**HATE THIS**
Animal		
Color		
Smell		
Word		
Weather		
Holiday		
Website		
Car		
Gadget		
Game		
Store or brand		
Teacher or leader		
City or state		

LOVE THIS	HATE THIS
Restaurant	
Night spot	
Sports team	
Athlete	
Movie	
Cartoon or comic strip	
Actor or actress	
Superhero or villain	
Book	
Magazine or newspaper	
Blog	
Writer	

Sports I play: _____

_____

Sports I watch: _____

_____

My favorite TV shows: _____

_____

_____

My hero(es): _____

_____

My most-prized possession: _____

_____

My oldest possession: _____

_____

In a typical week, I spend the most time doing these five things:

1. _____

2. _____

3. _____

4. _____

5. _____

In a typical weekend, I spend the most time doing these five things:

1. _____

2. _____

3. _____

4. _____

5. _____

Doodle (favorite shapes, a new signature, a tattoo you have or want, anything—it's totally up to you):

OVERALL

✍

My Life on the Whole

R E P O R T   C A R D

This is how satisfied I am with the various areas of my life right now:

N = NEEDS IMPROVEMENT	S = SATISFACTORY	E = EXCELLENT

____ My physical self   ____ My love life

____ My personality   ____ My home

____ My sense of style   ____ My work, school, other duties

____ My family   ____ My money

____ My friends

Notes on any *N*s above: _____

_____

_____

I'm quite proud of this *E* above: _____

_____

The most important thing in my life right now is: _____

_____

Cover of my autobiography (draw the cover and add a title):

Table of Contents (list the chapter topics in your story):

_____

_____

_____

_____

_____

_____

_____

_____

_____

_____

_____

_____

_____

If an automated phone survey asked me about the past year of my life, I'd:

___ Select 1 to repeat this past year over again—it was such a great year!

___ Select 2 to skip ahead to next year as fast as possible—this last one was the pits!

___ Select 3 to let time pass naturally—nothing special or terrible about this past year

___ Select 4 to speak to the operator—so much has happened, I need to talk it over with someone

Two positive changes or milestones I want in my life within _____ years:

1. _____

2. _____

This motto, saying, or lyric sums up my life right now: _____

_____

_____

One or two things I absolutely must do or see before I die:

_____

_____

Today's Date: _____

Dear Future Self,

_____

_____

_____

_____

_____

_____

_____

_____

_____

_____

_____

_____

_____

_____

_____

_____

_____

_____

_____

_____

_____

_____

_____

        _____

Kate and David Marshall
P.O. Box 6846
Moraga, CA. 94570–6846
www.marshallbooks.net